I learn by coloring - J'apprends en coloriant

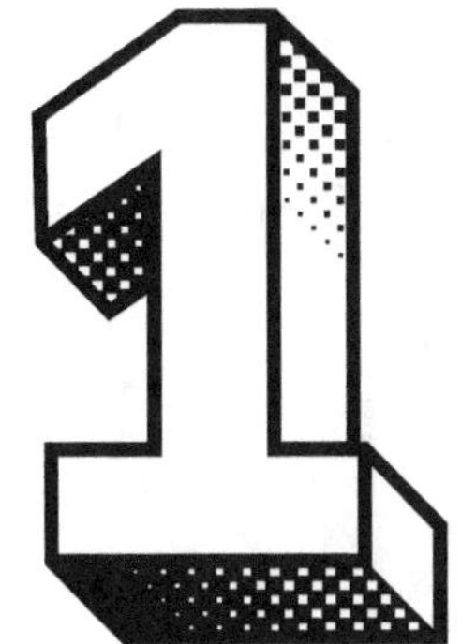

French - English

With this notebook, your child
will learn by coloring :
the first numbers,
the first words,
the first colors...
in English and French.
This learning is more effective
thanks to the coloring of words
in English and French.
Also, he can color the
illustrations which will help
him to understand better
by having fun.

I learn by coloring - J'apprends en coloriant

French - English

TROIS

THREE

French - English

QUATRE

French - English

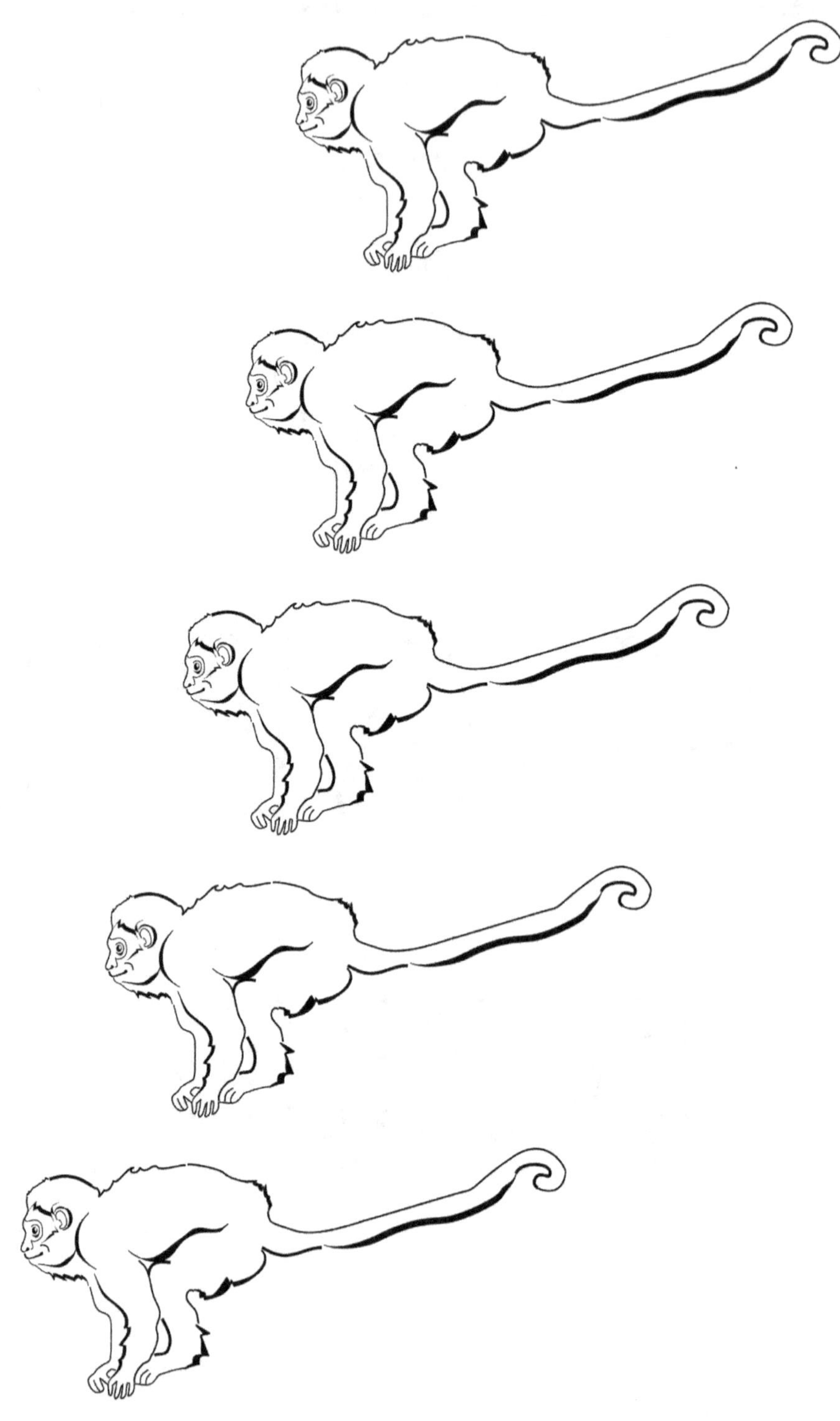

French - English

I learn by coloring - J'apprends en coloriant

SIX

SIX

French - English

I learn by coloring - J'apprends en coloriant

SEPT

SEVEN

French - English

I learn by coloring - J'apprends en coloriant

French - English

I learn by coloring - J'apprends en coloriant

French - English

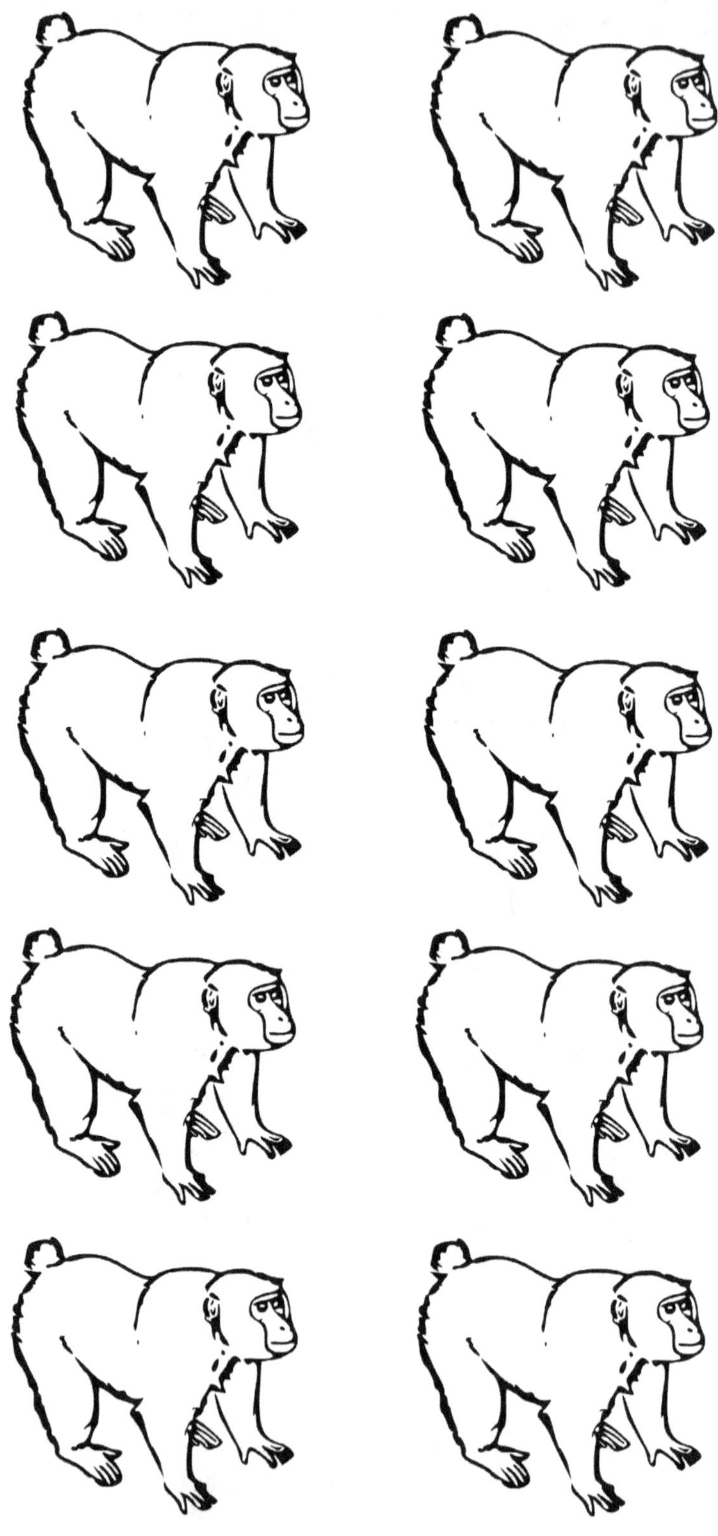

I learn by coloring - J'apprends en coloriant

DIX

TEN

French - English

I learn by coloring - J'apprends en coloriant

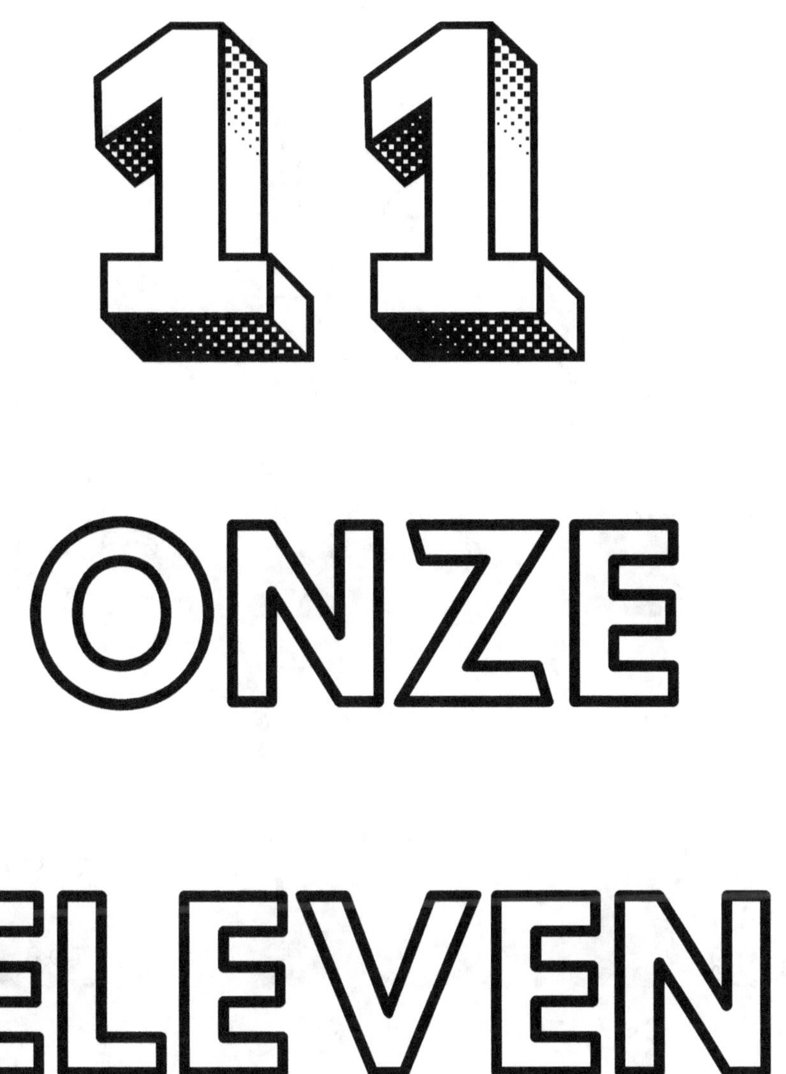

French - English

I learn by coloring - J'apprends en coloriant

DOUZE

TWELVE

French - English

TREIZE

THIRTEEN

French - English

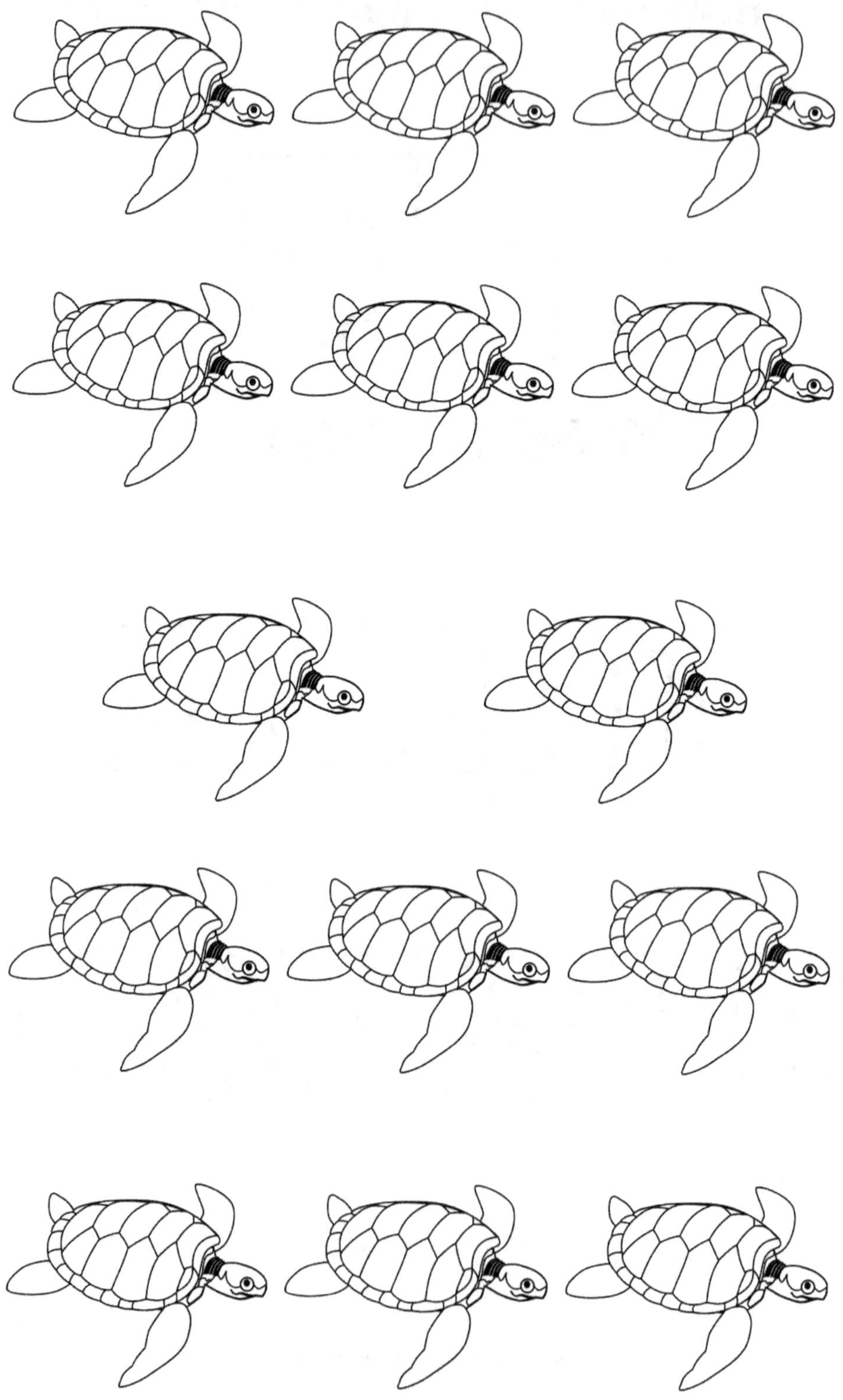

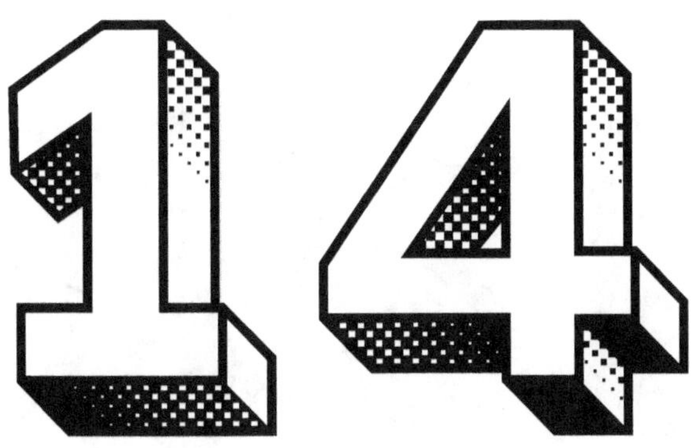

QUATORZE

FOURTEEN

French - English

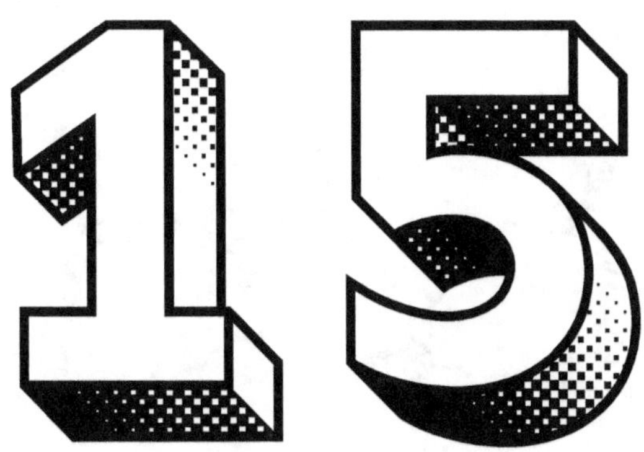

FIFTEEN

French - English

SEIZE

SIXTEEN

French - English

DIX-SEPT

SEVENTEEN

French - English

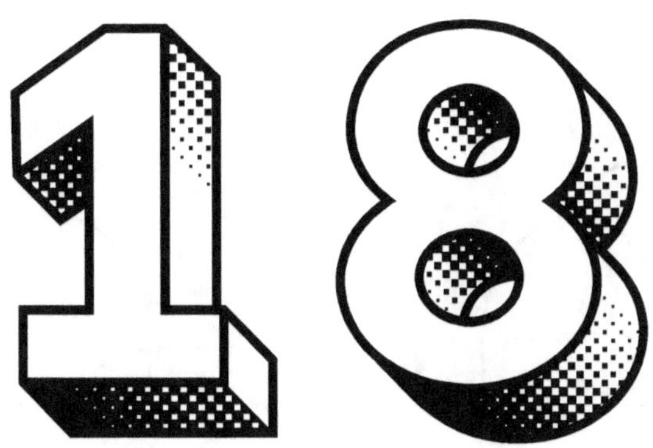

18

DIX-HUIT

EIGHTEEN

French - English

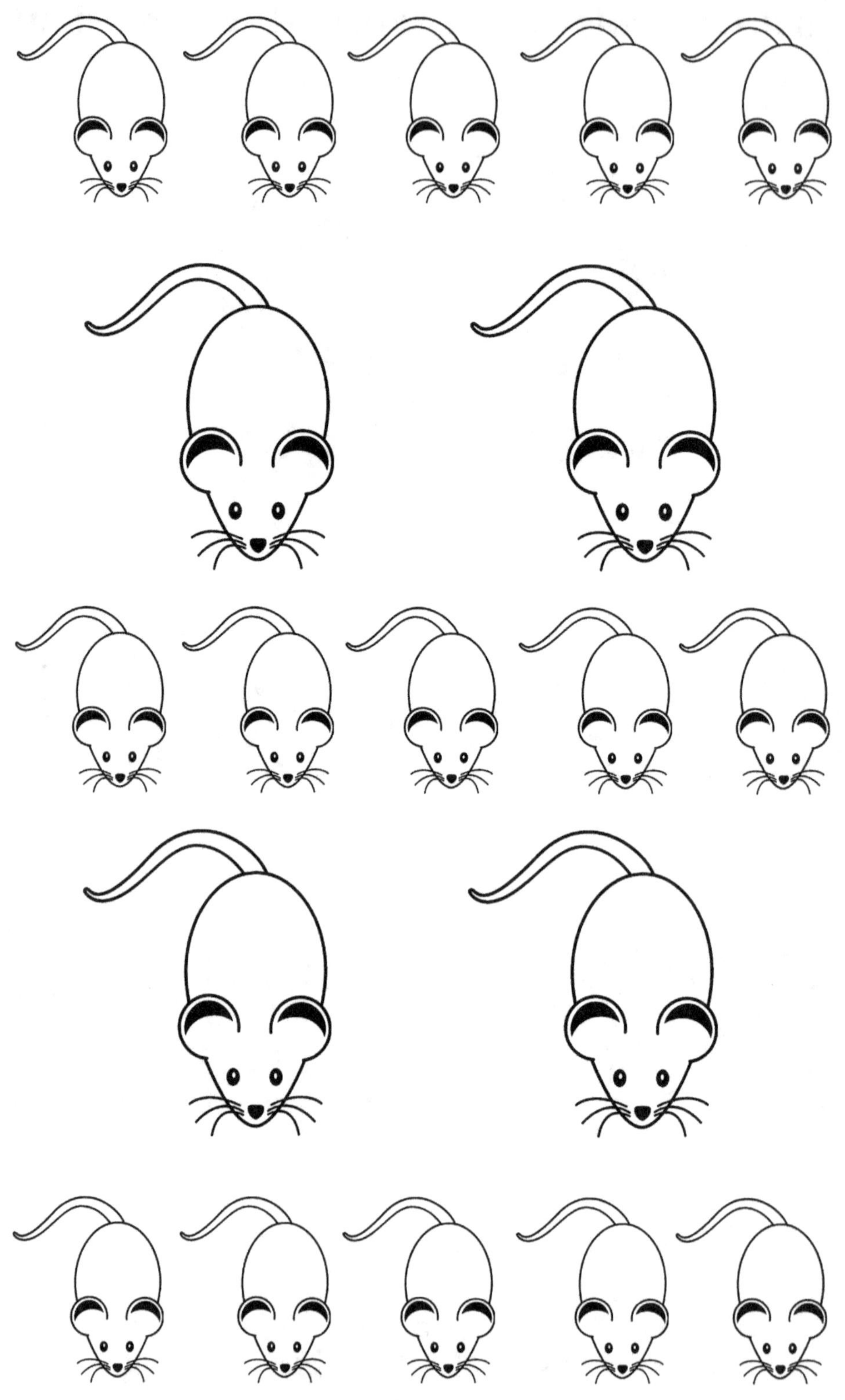

DIX-NEUF

NINETEEN

French - English

20

VINGT

TWENTY

French - English

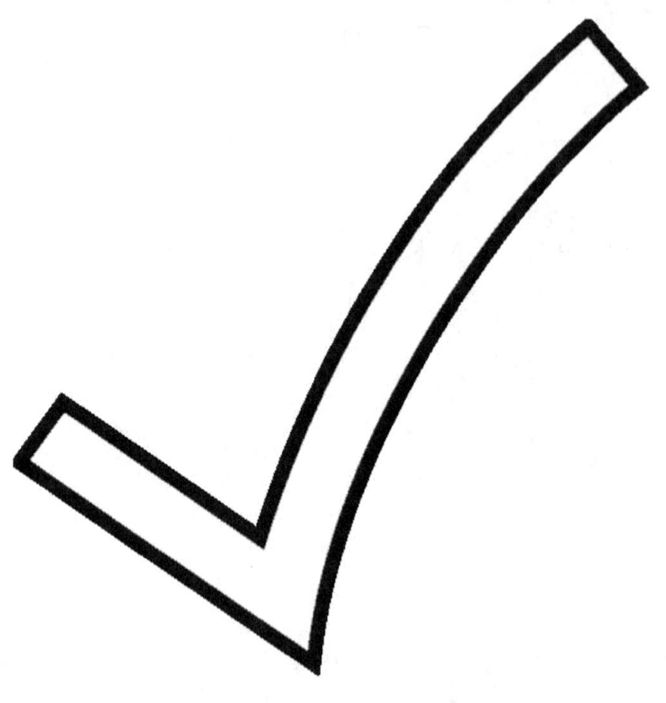

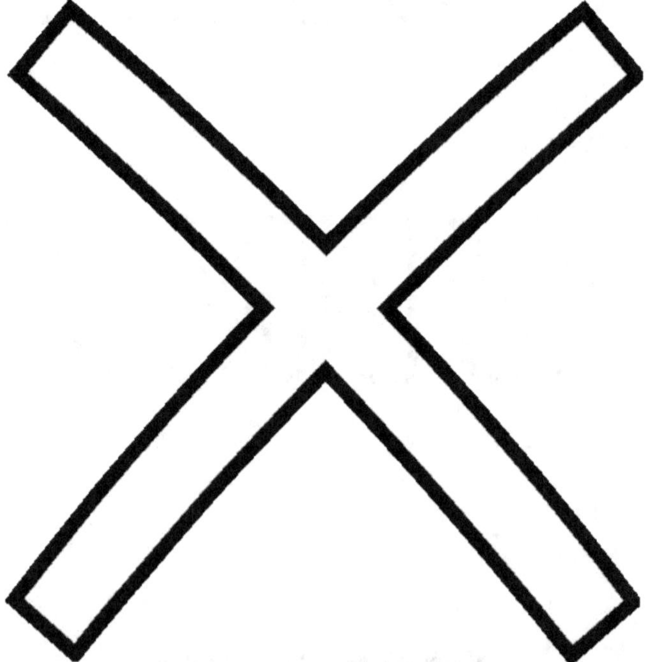

French - English

Draw a mother

MAMAN

MUM

MÈRE

MOTHER

French - English

Draw a dad

PAPA

DAD

PÈRE

FATHER

French - English

Draw a sister

Draw a brother

SOEUR

SISTER

FRÈRE

BROTHER

French - English

Draw an aunt

Draw an uncle

TATA

AUNT

TONTON

UNCLE

French - English

Draw a grandmother

Draw a grandfather

GRAND-MÈRE

GRANDMOTHER

GRAND-PÈRE

GRANDFATHER

French - English

Draw a girl

· ·

Draw a boy

FILLE

GIRL

GARCON

BOY

French - English

BÉBÉ

BABY

ENFANT

CHILD

French - English

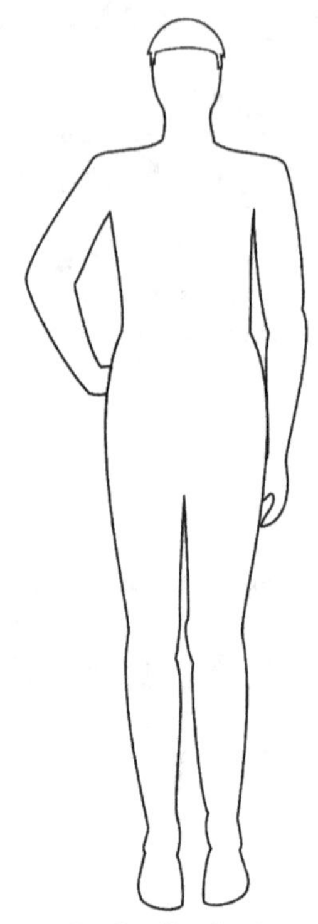

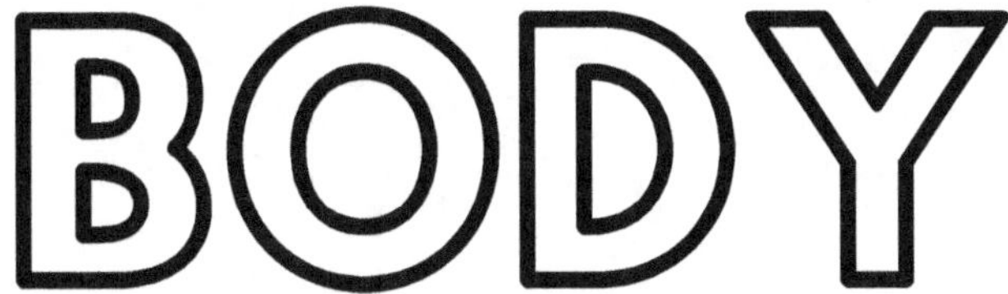

French - English

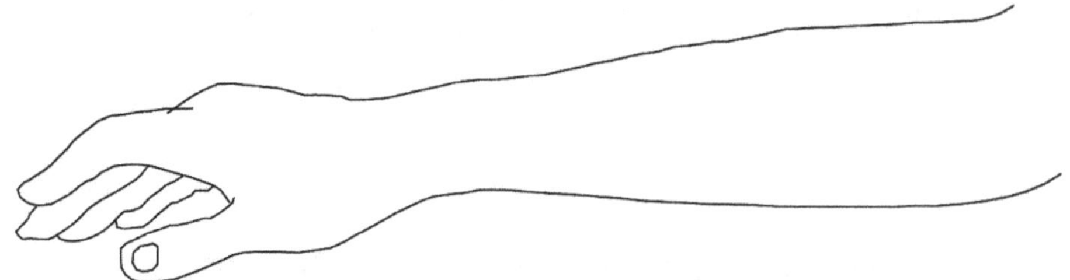

BRAS

ARM

MAIN

HAND

French - English

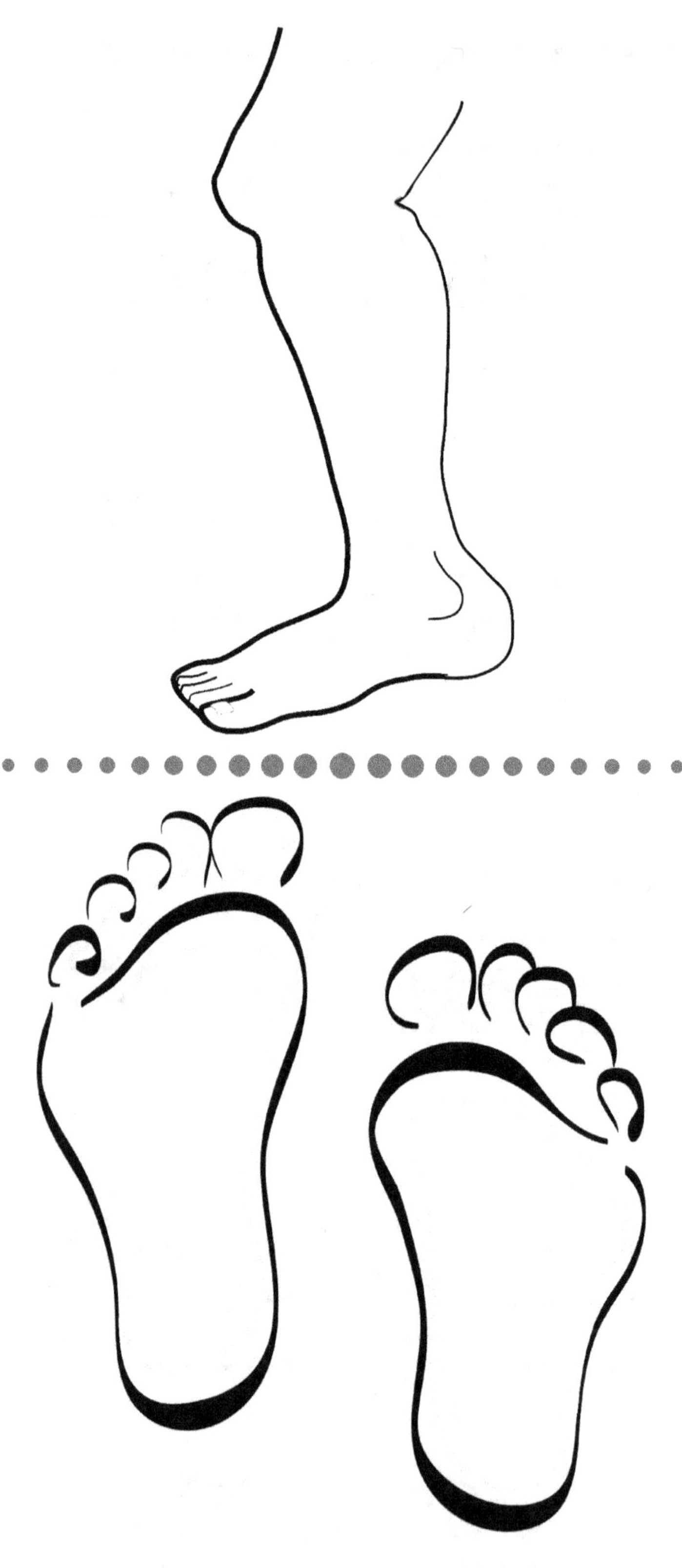

I learn by coloring - J'apprends en coloriant

JAMBE

LEG

PIED

FOOT

French - English

BLANC

WHITE

NOIR

BLACK

French - English

JAUNE

YELLOW

ORANGE

ORANGE

French - English

ROUGE

RED

BLEU

BLUE

French - English

VERT

GREEN

MARRON

BROWN

French - English

I learn by coloring - J'apprends en coloriant

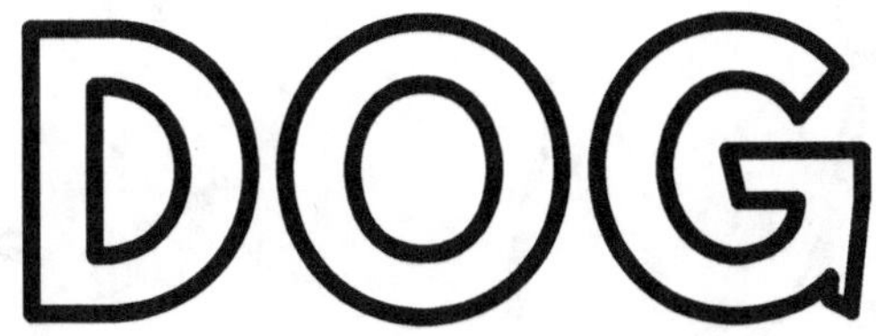

French - English

OISEAU

BIRD

LAPIN

RABBIT

French - English

EAU

WATER

PAIN

BREAD

French - English

POMME

APPLE

ORANGE

ORANGE

French - English

BANANE

BANANA

FRAISE

STRAWBERRY

French - English

MAISON

HOME

VOITURE

CAR

French - English

TABLE

TABLE

CHAISE

CHAIR

French - English